Our Global Commun

What Is A Community?

Rebecca Rissman

Heinemann Library
Chicago, Illinois

www.heinemannraintree.com
Visit our website to find out
more information about
Heinemann-Raintree books.

To order:
☎ Phone 888-454-2279
💻 Visit www.heinemannraintree.com
   to browse our catalog and order online.

©2009 Heinemann Library
an imprint of Capstone Global Library, LLC
Chicago, Illinois

Edited by Rebecca Rissman, Siân Smith, and Charlotte Guillain
Designed by Kimberly Miracle and Joanne Malivoire
Picture research by Elizabeth Alexander
Originated by Capstone Global Library
Printed and bound in China by Leo Paper Products Ltd

13 12 11 10 09
10 9 8 7 6 5 4 3 2 1

Library of Congress Cataloging-in-Publication Data

Rissman, Rebecca.
  What is a community? / Rebecca Rissman.
      p. cm.
  Includes bibliographical references and index.
  ISBN 978-1-4329-3259-6 (hc)
  ISBN 978-1-4329-3260-2 (pb)
  1. Communities--Juvenile literature. I. Title.
  HM756.R57 2009
  307--dc22
                            2008055314

Acknowledgments

The author and publishers are grateful to the following for
permission to reproduce copyright material: Alamy pp. **4 left**
(© Danita Delimont), **4 middle** (© Keren Su/China Span),
5 left (© Blend Images), **7 top left** (© Big Cheese Photo
LLC), **16** (© Imagestate Media Partners Limited - Impact
Photos), **17 middle** (© Image Source Pink), **19 bottom right**
(© db images); Corbis pp. **4 right** (© Vince Streano), **10** (©
Owen Franken), **11 middle** (© Roman Soumar), **11 right** (©
Christophe Boisvieux), **14** (© Tom Nebbia), **15 bottom left**
(© Rick D'Elia), **15 top left** (© Keith Wood), **15 top right**
(© Martin Alipaz/epa), **17 right** (© Tim Pannell), **18** (© Jim
Craigmyle), **21** (© Fancy/Veer); Getty Images pp. **7 right**
(Chris Clinton/Taxi), **9 top left** (Robert E Daemmrich/Stone);
Panos pp. **5 right**, **6** (Giacomo Pirozzi), **7 bottom left**
(Fernando Moleres), **9 bottom left** (Eric Miller), **11 left** (Mark
Henley), **15 bottom right** (Andrew Testa), **17 left** (G.M.B.
Akash), **19 top right** (Chris Sattlberger), **20 left** (Penny
Tweedie); Photolibrary pp. **8** (Patrick Luethy/age fotostock),
9 right (Digital Vision), **13 left**, **13 middle** (Mark Bowie/
Animals Animals), **19 left** (© Per Magnus Persson/Johner);
Still Pictures pp. **13 right** (© Andreas Sterzing / VISUM), **20
right** (© Fred Bruemmer).

Cover photograph of Samburu people in Kenya reproduced
with permission of Photolibrary (Winfried Wisniewski/ age
fotostock). Back cover photograph of a pop musician in a
recording studio reproduced with permission of Photolibrary
(Digital Vision).

We would like to thank Nancy Harris and Adriana Scalise for
their help in the preparation of this book.

Every effort has been made to contact copyright holders of
any material reproduced in this book. Any omissions will
be rectified in subsequent printings if notice is given to the
publisher.

Some words are shown in bold, **like this.** They are
explained in "Words to Know" on page 23.

Contents

About this series

Books in the **Our Global Community** series introduce children to many different elements of our global community. Use this book to stimulate discussion about different types of communities, and how people all over the world have things in common.

People Around the World

People live in different places around the world.
People live in different **communities**. A community
is a group of people.

But people around the world are also alike. People around the world do **similar** things.

Going to School

A school is a **community**. People go to schools around the world. Teachers go to schools to teach. Students go to schools to learn.

There are different types of schools around the world.
Some schools teach art. Some schools teach dance.
Some schools teach many things.

Making Music

People in different **communities** make music. They make music in many ways.

People make music with **instruments**. People make music with their hands and voices. People make music with computers.

Shopping at Markets

People in different **communities** go to markets around the world. People go to markets to buy things. People go to markets to sell things.

Markets can be different around the world. Some markets are **outdoors**. Some markets are **indoors**. Some markets are very big. Some markets are very small.

Wearing Clothes

People wear clothes around the world. People wear clothes to **protect** their bodies.

uniform

People wear different clothes to do different things. Some clothes are for swimming. Some clothes are for special parties. Some clothes are for work.

Working on Farms

Farmers work on farms around the world. Farmers in different places around the world grow different types of food. Farmers sell their food for others to eat.

Farms can grow different things around the world. Farmers grow fruits to sell. Farmers grow vegetables to sell. Farmers grow **grains** to sell. Farmers raise animals, too.

Playing Games

People play games around the world. People play games to have fun. People play games to learn.

People can play different types of games around the world. Some games are played in school. Some games are played at home. Some games are played outside.

Families at Home

A family is a **community**. People have families around the world. Some families live together. Some people in the same family live in different places.

Families live in different types of homes around the world. Some families live in homes that stay in one place. Some families live in homes that can move.

Similar and Different

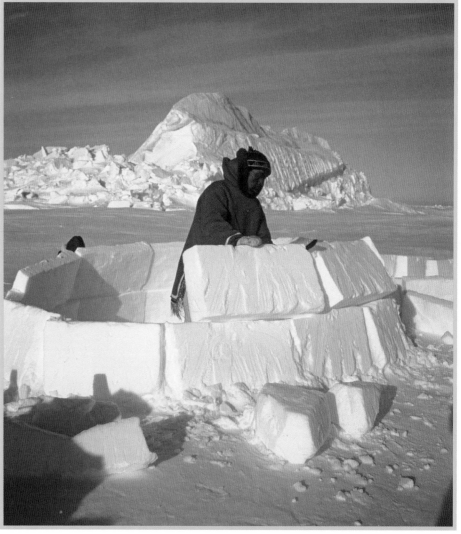

There are different types of **communities** around the world. People in different communities may live in different places and do different things.

But people around the world are **similar**, too.
We are all part of one really big community.
We all live together on planet Earth.

Different Communities

People can be part of lots of different communities at the same time. Here are some **communities** you might be part of:

- a family
- a group of friends
- the school you go to
- a club you go to
- a **religion** you believe in
- the neighborhood you live in
- the country you live in
- the planet we live on

We all live on the planet Earth and this makes us all part of one really big community. This is called our **global** community.

Words to Know

community
group of people that have something in common. A community can be a group of people who live, work, play, or do other things together.

grains
seeds that people and other animals eat. Oats and wheat are grains.

global
to do with the whole world

indoors
inside a building

instrument
something people use to make music

outdoors
outside

protect
keep safe

religion
believing in a god or gods. There are many different religions and people who belong to different religions believe different things.

similar
like something else

uniform
set of clothes people have to wear for their job or for school which makes them look the same. For example police officers may all wear the same uniform so that people can tell who they are.

Index

Note to Parents and Teachers

Before reading

Tell children that a community is a group of people. There are many different and similar communities around the world. Some communities across the world are schools, families, neighborhoods, religious groups, and work places. Ask children to think about and share some of the different communities they are part of.

After reading

- Give the children a selection of magazines and ask them to cut out pictures that show different communities. Help the children to sort the pictures, make up a collage, and give each collage a title. For example, "Families are Different" or "Music across the World."

- Ask children to draw a picture or write about one of their favorite communities. Children can share their pictures and stories in pairs and discuss why the community they have chosen is important.

- Divide children into different communities – a family, a school, a sports club, and people who work together in a grocery store. Tell children to make a list with their group about things their community does together. Each group can then make a performance that helps people to learn about that community. Children can use props, costumes, and pictures to aid in their performances.